Tacoshop22rl

Seth Rasporich

Tacoshop22rl

Radical Bookshop and Press
4838 Richard Road SW, Suite 300
Calgary, AB T3E 6L1

BIO009000 - Biography and Autobiography, Personal Memoir

February 28, 2023

Editors: Lexie Angelo
Cover Design: Lexie Angelo

ISBN-13: 978-1-990201-13-4

Printed in the United States

Chris "Taco" Johnson

Contents

Tacoshop22rl

Tacoshop22rl was the same height and weight as Lebron James. Six-feet and eight inches weighing in at two-hundred and eighty pounds. A towering black man with freckles and an orange beard. I wasn't small by any means, Keanu Reeves-sized to be exact; I still identified as tall. I lived in cold-as-hell Canada; Tacoshop22rl lived in sunny San Diego.

We'd never meet in person.

We met online years ago in game of Rainbow Six Siege. I had a particularly good game that night; I'd killed nineteen enemies and hadn't died once. Throughout the game, a deep voice in my headset cheered me on.

"He slick w' it huh? Pops really finna cop the 19k."

After the game, Tacoshop22rl messaged me, asked if I would 'carry his ass?' I accepted. Taco and I played long into the night. He never let go of my lucky display of video game prowess. Even on my losing streaks. If any of my friends talked down on my gaming skills, Taco rushed to my defense.

"Better watch your mouth, you need to understand who you're talkin' to, he got the 19K bro."

At the same time, I'd just been fired from a mall olive oil store because I wasn't passionate enough about my sales. I was going through my first major heartbreak and my sociology degree was beginning to feel remedial. I lived with four other boys at the time. They had all landed internships in their fields of finance and computer science. We led similar lives: a nightly routine of blunts, Domino's pizza, and PlayStation until our vision vibrated. In the morning, my roommates went to work in their businessman costumes. I continued the video games, cold pizza, and lung-busters throughout the day. They had their careers to distract them from the dread of their early twenties, I had a PlayStation in a laundry room.

Taco sent me memes and videos at an unprecedented rate. Here was this actual giant of a man I'd only played games with for a single night documenting his entire life. He lived in a 300 square foot concrete apartment furnished with a PlayStation, a George Foreman grill, and a resin bong.

"Hop on for sum squad shit, Pops," Taco messaged me daily.

He and I played together whole days at a time because neither of us had much going on. I liked playing with him because he was so personable. He was open about his bi-polar disorder and the disability pay that allowed him his sedentary lifestyle. He made quick pals with every gamer we encountered and had cultivated a small community of online friends. I could log on to find him playing with ChickenNugget, an autistic 12-year-old boy from Ohio; or ArmedNotLegged, an amputee father of three in the

Yukon. It didn't take long before he became close with all my roommates. We had a running joke that Taco had become our sixth roommate. Whether his deep-ass voice was coming through the TV, our headsets, or FaceTime, he was virtually living with us.

"What's Tacoshop22rl stand for?" one of my roommates asked.

"I don't wanna talk 'bout that right now," Taco said, going quiet.

We continued gaming. Later that night he messaged me privately, 'Can we talk, Pops?'

"For sure bro," I replied.

"RL stands for rich life. My homie Richie got stabbed two years back, I don't like gettin' into it. Tell the homies so they know. Twenty-two was his basketball number," Taco told me.

I didn't know what to say, his candidness with us white Canadian boys he had never met surprised me.

Years passed and our routine stayed the same, although we played different games. Sometimes we didn't even play games we'd just log on to chew the fat. We came to know Taco's friends as well; our chats became a blend of my friends in Canada and Taco's in California. I'd boot up my PlayStation to join a party chat with my older brother, an automotive engineer in Calgary, and Taco's friend Dre. Dre explained the difference between his time spent in prisons versus county-jails. In county-jails, he got a TV. Dre was a good kid; I couldn't help but think that if he'd gone to school in Canada, he probably would have had an educational assistant as opposed to a prison guard.

Taco also grew close with my brother because he had wanted to be a mechanic and buy a motorcycle someday. They talked about Taco's dream bike, a BMW M1000, in detail that went well beyond my expertise. We'd FaceTime Taco on Christmas and New Year's because he was a member of our large digital family. We sent Christmas cards. I once had to talk Taco out of mailing me a card that he'd slipped a sheet of California's finest cannabis wax in.

I joked that he was my online therapist. Only better because he, unlike a therapist, was not a paid friend. After a cut-throat breakup, Taco was the first person I called because he didn't pull any punches.

"I mean bro, if shits this hard, sumn's just tryna tell ya it aint how its 'sposed to be. You a funny ass dude, you got style. Trust me, Pops you goin' be right. You got the 19k bro, you don't gotta cry in the club bout' this," Taco said.

All I needed to hear. He was the first responder on three different heartbreaks, two evictions, countless firings, and four university dropouts. My eternal losing streak.

"Me and the boys were talking about taking a road trip in the summer, maybe we could come down to Cali. Could we crash on your floor?" I asked him. He went quiet on the headset.

"Yeah, that'd be cool," he said, pausing.

He cleared his throat, "I just want y'all to know I'm not this cool or funny in person, like I get anxious."

I told him that was fine, we didn't care. I never did make it down due to work, money, and COVID-19.

He was my biggest cheerleader, genuinely thrilled whenever I told him about a new job or girlfriend. And vice-versa. He called me before his first ever job interview at Zara's, a fashion clothing store.

"I need advice on how to talk that big business shit y'all on, help me sound all professional n' shit."

We laughed.

He called me after he met an online girl. I was pretty sure he was being cat-fished, but I cheered him on anyway. When that fell apart, he contacted me to draft a sincere break-up message.

There was a stupid amount of excitement in the group chat when he flooded our inboxes with pictures of his first motorcycle, a BMW M1000. He had gotten into mechanics school; we were all stoked.

Later I received the 'Can we talk, Pops?' message followed by 'I had a bad few days. Got kicked out of school.'

He had inadvertently worn shorts to school. His white female instructor told him he had to change his clothes.

"You can't do mechanics in shorts," she had said.

He explained to that if he went home to change, he'd miss the whole day.

"I won't wear them again," he'd promised.

"You're scaring me," she'd said.

When he'd risen from his desk, she picked up the phone and called the police. Taco knew what was coming. He'd seen it with Dre. He got on his bike and left before the police had arrived. He had received an expulsion letter that night; his crime, being a six-eight black man in accidental shorts.

Over the next year we talked less and less, but that was a good thing. We had less time for video games now because Taco had a real-life girlfriend. He'd finished mechanics school elsewhere and got a big-boy job at Dodge. I lived with my girlfriend and was working long days in film. Our somber 'Can we talk?' messages faded. We were both doing okay. Now, we messaged each other with good news. Taco sent pictures of himself at cookouts and sushi dinners surrounded by real-life friends.

13

A far cry from the concrete-apartment shut-in I'd met six years earlier. We'd stopped smoking weed and had real things going on in our lives. Taco didn't have to worry about being cool or funny anymore; he had grown into the life he wanted. We kept in touch less like gamers, more like old friends.

Two weeks ago, he had messaged me to play online mini golf. Despite my 12-hour-day on set, I made the time to play. Taco joked about being the best man at my wedding.

"The pics'd be crazy huh? Buncha skinny ass white boys, yknow farmers n' accountants n' shit. My big ass beside y'all, head out the frame."

I wished we could've.

Last night, I received a message from an account I didn't recognize. It went to my spam folder that I rarely checked. Curious, before I went to bed, I opened it.

"Hi – I remember he would talk about you – please send this to your chat." The message was from Taco's girlfriend. Attached was a screenshot of Taco's freckled face and orange beard followed by a link to a news site. The headline:

1 Man Dies in Motorcycle Accident in Mission Beach.

The article was short. At 9:40 p.m., a 25-year-old-man ran a red-light on a BMW M1000 and collided fatally with a Volkswagen Tiguan. The woman in the Tiguan complained of pain in her neck and back. My friend, Tacoshop22rl was dead. The article was followed by cold-hearted comments:

> *What'd he expect running a red light??*

> *I hope the woman is okay, the man knew what he was getting into on a bike that fast.*

> *Like leaving Post it Notes on the grave of a fallen soldier.*

He shoulda been a better shot.

The dirge of the digital world.

I opened our group chat to tell the homies. Taco had liked my brother's daily Wordle score the day before. I received the message from his girlfriend that he was dead at 9:52 pm. Sixteen-hundred miles away, but in my head we were in the same room not thirty-two minutes ago.

Over the coming days, I tried to track down our mutual gaming friends. How to tell ChickenNugget, the now 18-year-old autistic boy from Ohio? I never sent the message. I messaged ArmedNotLegged, the legless father in the Yukon. I messaged Dre, he didn't reply. I hoped that he wasn't in prison again, or if he was, it was the county-jail with TV's. I wrote a letter to Taco's mother and girlfriend, uncertain what details I should include since I had never met either of them. Did I bring up the cannabis-filled birthday card? The catfish girlfriend? What if they were Catholic? I wanted them to know how much Taco affected my Canadian life over the last six years.

As I wrote — I felt selfish. Here was a girl who'd lost her lover, and a mother, her son. How could I, the gamer who'd lost a squad-mate, possibly relate to their grief? In my mind, I had no right to be upset. Taco and I had never even occupied the same room. Did that matter? I had nowhere to put my sadness. Taco would've been my first call, 'Can we talk?' On the scale of one-to-ten, I had no idea where to place the loss of my virtual-best-friend. It felt like ten. If one of my close friends from high school had died instead, would I allow myself proper grief? If a coworker I saw every day on set had died, at least there would be a funeral to attend, and the people around me would understand my grief because they'd have witnessed our physical proximity.

I didn't know how to feel.

My university dropouts, my failed relationships, my career suicides. Taco's death. Losing streaks. The thing I kept coming back to.

Taco's deep-ass voice coming through my headset:

"If you quit every time you lose. Bro, how the fuck you ever goin' win?"

ACKNOWLEDGEMENTS

Many thanks to Lee Kvern, I read her books as a child and I never would've put pen to page without her work.

ABOUT THE AUTHOR

Seth Rasporich is a Canadian student in what feels to be his one thousandth year of University, never completing a full degree. He has dropped out of nearly every major university in Alberta. He has worked as a sculptor and painter for film, but mostly as a barista for the loneliest of mall shoppers. His work ranges from creative non-fiction to screenplays which he swallows whole before completion.

SPECIAL THANKS

Calgary Arts Development

Calgary Public Library

IngramSpark

CPSIA information can be obtained
at www.ICGtesting.com
Printed in the USA
JSHW021150030323
38330JS00010BB/176